DRAWINGS IN THE FOGG MUSEUM OF ART

A CRITICAL CATALOGUE BY AGNES MONGAN AND PAUL J. SACHS

ITALIAN, GERMAN FLEMISH, DUTCH, FRENCH, SPANISH, MISCELLANEOUS SCHOOLS

VOLUME II : PLATES

HARVARD–RADCLIFFE FINE ARTS SERIES

LONDON : GEOFFREY CUMBERLEGE
OXFORD UNIVERSITY PRESS

DRAWINGS
IN THE FOGG MUSEUM OF ART

BY

AGNES MONGAN
Keeper of Drawings

AND

PAUL J. SACHS
Professor of Fine Arts, Harvard University

CAMBRIDGE, MASSACHUSETTS
HARVARD UNIVERSITY PRESS
1946

q 741
f H334
V. 2

Second Edition

THE REPRODUCTIONS IN THIS VOLUME HAVE BEEN MADE AND PRINTED BY
THE MERIDEN GRAVURE CO., MERIDEN, CONN., U. S. A.

PRINTED AT THE HARVARD UNIVERSITY PRINTING OFFICE
CAMBRIDGE, MASSACHUSETTS, U. S. A.

LIST OF ILLUSTRATIONS

ITALIAN, XIV AND XV CENTURIES

Fig. 1 $9\frac{5}{8}$ x 9 (recto)

ITALIAN, XIV CENTURY

Fig. 2

9⅝ x 9 (verso)

ITALIAN, XIV CENTURY

Fig. 3   Actual size

SCHOOL OF FRA ANGELICO

Fig. 4   Actual size

SCHOOL OF FRA ANGELICO

Fig. 5 $3\frac{3}{4}$ (l.) or $8\frac{1}{4}$ (rt.) x 12

JACOPO BELLINI

Fig. 6

$8\frac{5}{8} \times 12\frac{3}{8}$

VITTORE CARPACCIO

Fig. 7

$9\frac{7}{8} \times 8\frac{1}{8}$

SCHOOL OF LORENZO DI CREDI

Fig. 8   Actual size

BENOZZO GOZZOLI

Fig. 9 $7\frac{3}{4} \times 5\frac{1}{4}$

CARLO CRIVELLI (?)

Fig. 10   10 x 4½

SCHOOL OF FERRARA

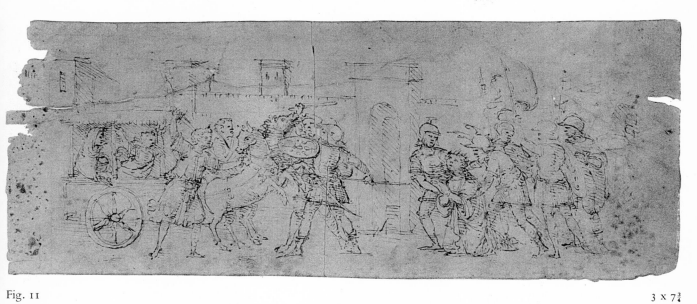

Fig. 11

3 x 7¾

FLORENTINE SCHOOL, XV CENTURY

Fig. 12

Actual size

FLORENTINE SCHOOL, XV CENTURY

Fig. 13   11 x 5⅝

FLORENTINE SCHOOL, XV CENTURY

Fig. 14 $5\frac{3}{4} \times 4\frac{5}{16}$

FLORENTINE SCHOOL, XV CENTURY

Fig. 15 $7\frac{1}{2} \times 9\frac{3}{4}$

ITALIAN, XV CENTURY

Fig. 16   15 x 11 (recto)

VINCENZO FOPPA (?)

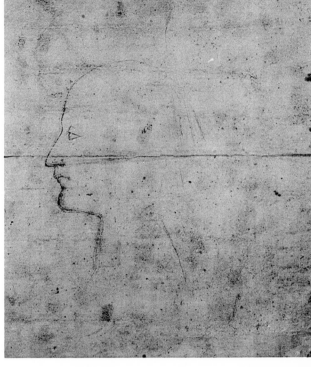

Fig. 17   15 x 11 (verso)

VINCENZO FOPPA (?)

Fig. 18 $8\frac{7}{16} \times 6\frac{13}{16}$

BENOZZO GOZZOLI

Fig. 19 $4\frac{7}{8} \times 7\frac{5}{8}$

COPY AFTER BENOZZO GOZZOLI

Fig. 20 $8\frac{3}{4} \times 7\frac{1}{2}$

FILIPPINO LIPPI

Fig. 21   9⅞ x 7¼ (recto)

FILIPPINO LIPPI

Fig. 22 $9\frac{7}{8} \times 7\frac{1}{8}$ (verso)

FILIPPINO LIPPI

Fig. 23

10⅝ x 7½ (recto)

LOMBARD, XV CENTURY

Fig. 24 $10\frac{1}{8} \times 7\frac{1}{2}$ (verso)

LOMBARD, XV CENTURY

ANDREA MANTEGNA

Fig. 26

$11\frac{3}{4} \times 8\frac{?}{?}$

PIETRO PERUGINO

Fig. 27

$11\frac{3}{4} \times 7\frac{3}{4}$ (recto)

PIETRO PERUGINO

Fig. 28

SCHOOL OF PERUGINO

Fig. 29 $10\frac{7}{16} \times 5\frac{1}{2}$

SCHOOL OF PERUGINO

Fig. 30

9⅝ x 7

BERNARDINO PINTURICCHIO

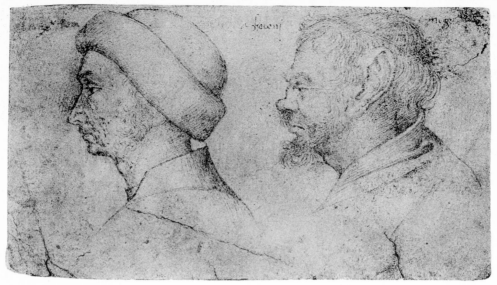

Fig. 31   Actual size

ANTONIO PISANELLO (?)

Fig. 32 $7\frac{1}{2} \times 6\frac{1}{4}$

SCHOOL OF PISANELLO

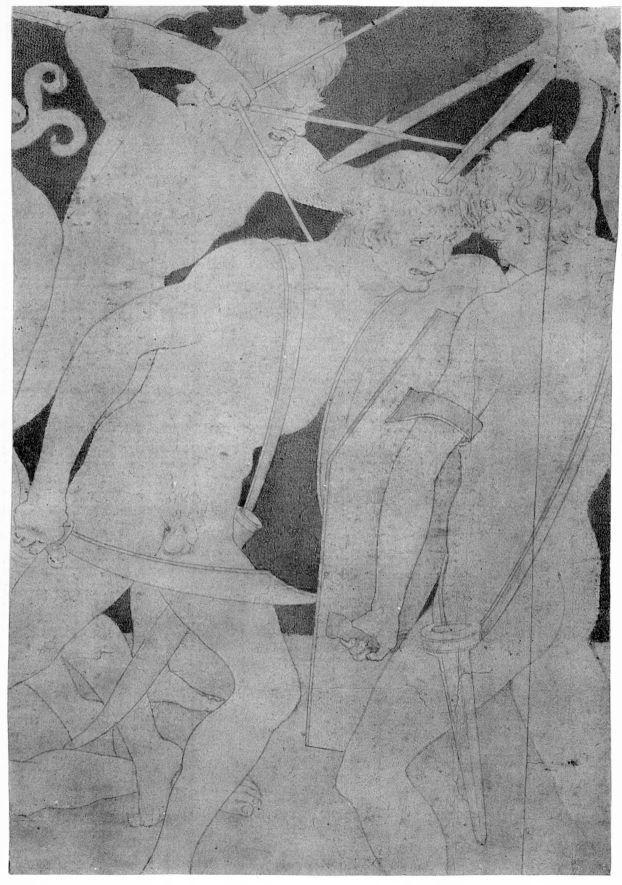

Fig. 33

$10\frac{5}{8} \times 7\frac{1}{16}$

ANTONIO DEL POLLAIUOLO

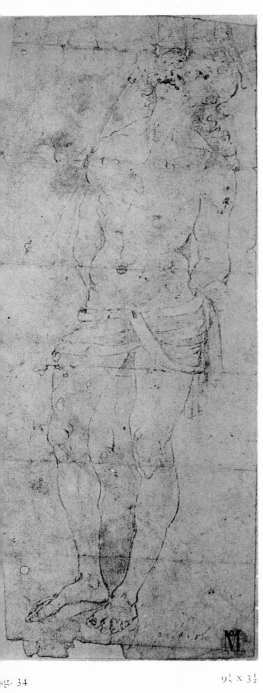

Fig. 35   7⅜ x 5½

MANNER OF JACOPO DEL SELLAIO

g. 34   9¼ x 3½

SCHOOL OF POLLAIUOLO

Fig. 36   Actual size

TUSCAN, XV CENTURY

Fig. 37   6¼ x 7¼

SCHOOL OF MANTEGNA

Fig. 38   9⅜ x 7¼

TUSCAN, XV CENTURY

Fig. 39   Actual size

UMBRO–FLORENTINE, XV CENTURY

Fig. 40   8⅞ x 4¾

VENETIAN, XV CENTURY

Fig. 41   10¼ x 7

VENETIAN, XV CENTURY

Fig. 42

VENETIAN, XV CENTURY

ITALIAN, XVI CENTURY

Fig. 43 $8\frac{7}{16} \times 8\frac{1}{2}$

MARIOTTO ALBERTINELLI (?)

Fig. 44 $8\frac{1}{8} \times 5\frac{7}{8}$

GIOVANNANTONIO SOGLIANI

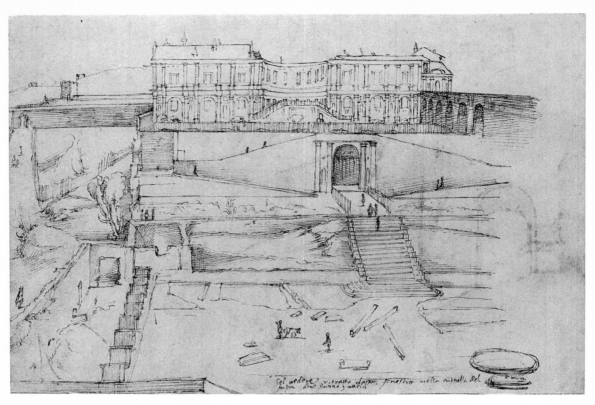

Fig. 45   9½ x 13½ (recto)

Fig. 46   9½ x 13½ (verso)

BARTOLOMEO AMMANATI (?)

Fig. 47 $15\frac{5}{8} \times 9\frac{3}{8}$

GIOVANNI BANDINI

Fig. 48

$5\frac{5}{16} \times 7\frac{5}{8}$

FRA BARTOLOMMEO

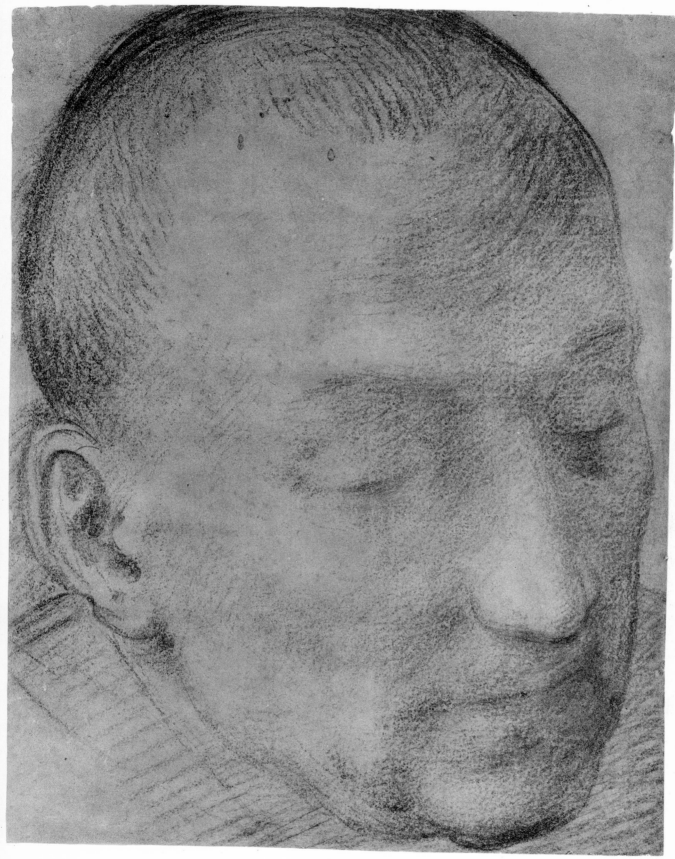

Fig. 49

Actual size

FRA BARTOLOMMEO

Fig. 50 $7\frac{5}{8}$ x $9\frac{5}{8}$ (recto)

FRA BARTOLOMMEO

Fig. 51 $9\frac{5}{8}$ x $7\frac{5}{8}$ (verso)

FRA BARTOLOMMEO

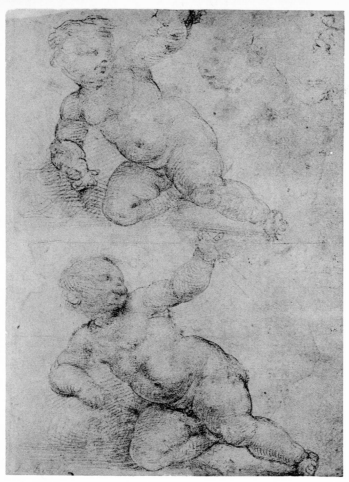

Fig. 52   11⅛ x 7⅞ (verso)

FRA BARTOLOMMEO

Fig. 53   7⅞ x 11⅛ (recto)

FRA BARTOLOMMEO

Fig. 54 $9\frac{1}{2} \times 7\frac{1}{2}$ (recto)

SCHOOL OF FRA BARTOLOMMEO

Fig. 55 $7\frac{1}{2} \times 9\frac{1}{2}$ (verso)

SCHOOL OF FRA BARTOLOMMEO

Fig. 56   Actual size

FEDERIGO BAROCCIO (?)

Fig. 57 $10\frac{9}{16} \times 7\frac{13}{16}$

DOMENICO BECCAFUMI

Fig. 58 $10 \times 6\frac{3}{4}$

DOMENICO BECCAFUMI

DOMENICO BECCAFUMI

Fig. 60

$12 \times 8\frac{1}{8}$

PARIS BORDONE (?)

Fig. 61 $15\frac{1}{8} \times 8\frac{7}{16}$

AGNOLO BRONZINO

Fig. 62

13 X

LUCA CAMBIASO

Fig. 63 $12\frac{1}{2} \times 8\frac{1}{2}$

LUCA CAMBIASO

Fig. 64 $8\frac{3}{4} \times 7\frac{15}{16}$

LUCA CAMBIASO

Fig. 65   9¾ x 15⅜

SCHOOL OF DOMENICO CAMPAGNOLA

Fig. 66   11⅛ x 10⅛

GIULIO CAMPI

Fig. 67 $13\frac{1}{4} \times 10\frac{1}{8}$

PIETRO FACCINI

Pietro Facini

Fig. 68

$12\frac{1}{2} \times 9$

PIETRO FACCINI

Fig. 69

$10\frac{1}{8} \times 7\frac{13}{16}$

GIOVANANTONIO DOSIO (?)

Fig. 70 $11\frac{3}{4} \times 8\frac{1}{4}$

GAUDENZIO FERRARI

Fig. 71

18⅞ x 12¼

GAUDENZIO FERRARI

Fig. 72   Actual size

SCHOOL OF LEONARDO

Fig. 73 $9\frac{1}{8} \times 6\frac{1}{4}$

LIBERALE DA VERONA

Fig. 74 $14\frac{5}{8} \times 10\frac{3}{8}$

BERNARDINO LUINI

Fig. 75 $11\frac{1}{2}$ x $8\frac{1}{4}$

BERNARDINO LUINI

Fig. 76 $6\frac{1}{4}$ x $6\frac{1}{4}$

SCHOOL OF MICHELANGELO

Fig. 77   5¾ × 4

SCHOOL OF MICHELANGELO

Fig. 78   12¾ × 9½

RAFFAELLO DA MONTELUPO

Fig. 79 $11\frac{3}{8} \times 7\frac{5}{8}$

PALMA GIOVANE

Fig. 80   8 x 4¾

PARMIGIANINO (?)

Fig. 81   5⅛ x 6⅞

PARMIGIANINO

Fig. 82 $11\frac{1}{2} \times 7\frac{3}{8}$

JACOPO PONTORMO

Fig. 83 $17\frac{1}{8} \times 11\frac{1}{4}$

JACOPO PONTORMO

Fig. 84 Actual size

RAPHAEL (?)

Fig. 85

RAPHAEL

Fig. 86   6 x 9⅛ (verso)

RAPHAEL (?)

Fig. 87   7¹¹⁄₁₆ x 9¼

SCHOOL OF RAPHAEL

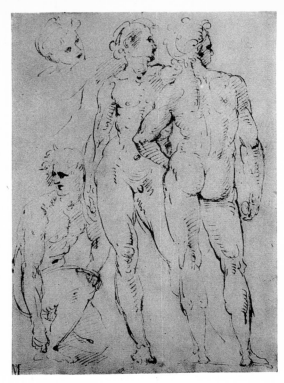

Fig. 88   9¾ x 6⅜

COPY AFTER RAPHAEL

Fig. 89   11¼ x 10⅜

COPY AFTER RAPHAEL

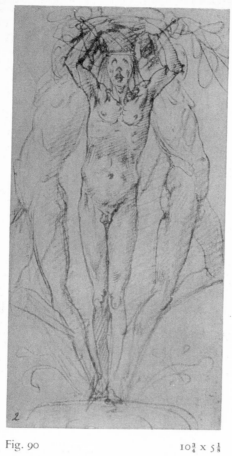

Fig. 90   10¾ x 5⅛

IL ROSSO (?)

Fig. 91   10¾ x 8⅛

SCHOOL OF IL ROSSO

Fig. 92 $15\frac{3}{4} \times 9\frac{5}{8}$

ANDREA DEL SARTO

Fig. 93 $11\frac{3}{4} \times 6\frac{1}{2}$

JACOPO TINTORETTO

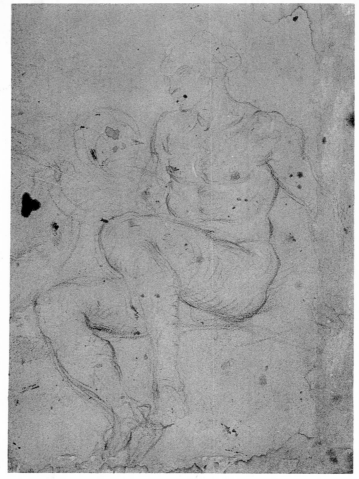

Fig. 94   15½ x 11 (recto)

JACOPO TINTORETTO

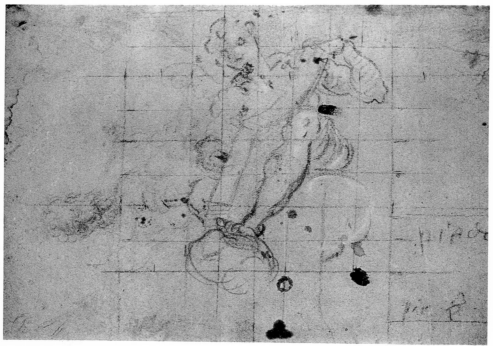

Fig. 95   11 x 15½ (verso)

JACOPO TINTORETTO

Fig. 96

$12\frac{3}{8} \times 8\frac{3}{4}$

JACOPO TINTORETTO

Fig. 97   17¾ x 10¾

JACOPO TINTORETTO

Fig. 98   15 x 9

JACOPO TINTORETTO

Fig. 99   4¾ x 8¾ (recto)

JACOPO TINTORETTO

Fig. 100   4¾ x 8¾ (verso)

JACOPO TINTORETTO

Fig. 101 $14\frac{5}{8} \times 13\frac{5}{8}$

PERINO DEL VAGA

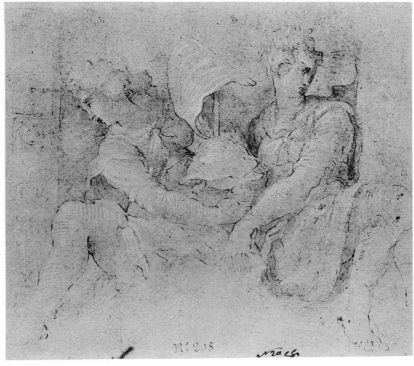

Fig. 102 $5\frac{3}{4} \times 6\frac{3}{8}$

PERINO DEL VAGA

Fig. 103 $7\frac{5}{16} \times 10\frac{5}{8}$

PERINO DEL VAGA (?)

Fig. 104

PERINO DEL VAGA

Fig. 105   8¾ x 8½

GIORGIO VASARI

Fig. 106   12¾ x 7⅜

GIORGIO VASARI

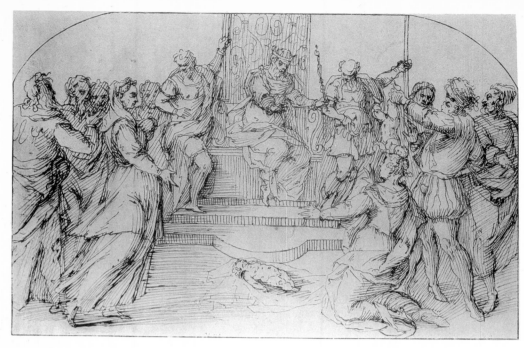

Fig. 107   8 x 12⅛

VENETIAN, XVI CENTURY

Fig. 108   Diam. 11¼

ANDREA VICENTINO

Fig. 109

11⅝ x 7⅞ (recto)

PAOLO VERONESE

Fig. 110

$11\frac{5}{8} \times 7\frac{7}{8}$ (verso)

PAOLO VERONESE

Fig. 111

$9\frac{3}{4} \times 7\frac{3}{4}$

PAOLO VERONESE

Fig. 112   7⅞ x 7⅛ (verso)

PAOLO VERONESE

Fig. 113   7⅞ x 7⅛ (recto)

PAOLO VERONESE

$16\frac{1}{4}$ x $12\frac{3}{4}$

PAOLO VERONESE (?)

Fig. 115   10 x 6⅝

PAOLO VERONESE (?)

116   9¼ x 16⅝

TADDEO ZUCCARO

Fig. 117   10⅝ x 8

FEDERIGO ZUCCARO

ITALIAN, XVII CENTURY

Fig. 118   20½ x 15

BOLOGNESE, XVII CENTURY

Fig. 119   16¼ x 10⅜

FRANCESCO BRIZZI

Fig. 120   14¾ x 10⅞

BOLOGNESE, XVII CENTURY

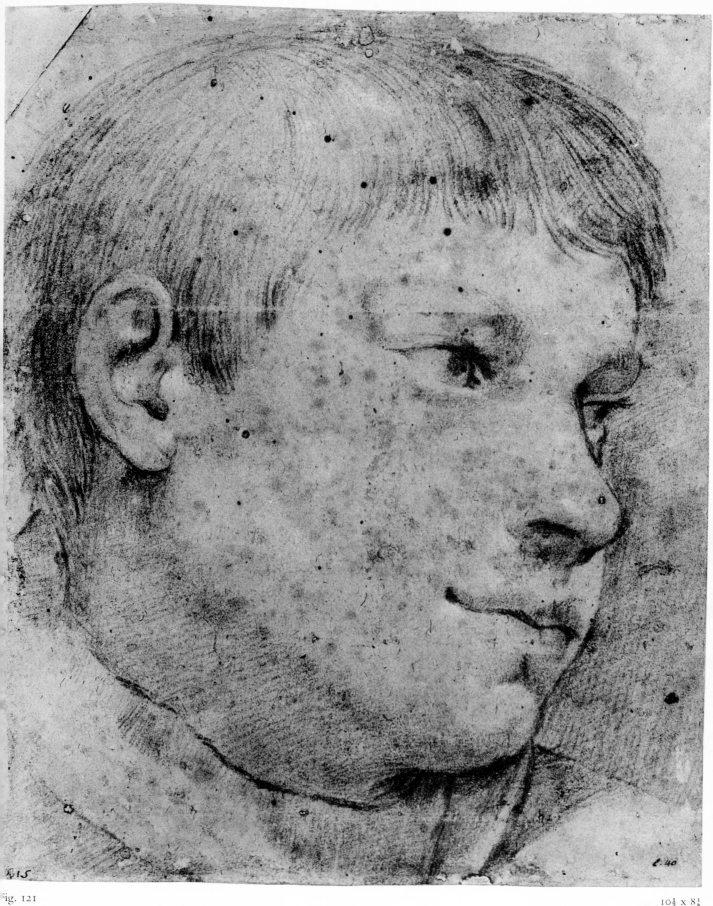

Fig. 121

$10\frac{1}{2} \times 8\frac{1}{8}$

ANNIBALE CARRACCI

Fig. 122

ANNIBALE CARRACCI

Fig. 123

$10\frac{7}{8} \times 16\frac{1}{8}$

BENEDETTO CASTIGLIONE

Fig. 124

$10\frac{1}{4} \times 15\frac{3}{4}$

BENEDETTO CASTIGLIONE

Fig. 125 $11\frac{1}{4} \times 1$

GIACOMO CAVEDONE

Fig. 126   8⅝ x 6¼

GIUSEPPE CESARI (D'ARPINO)

Fig. 127   11¼ x 10¼

CARLO CIGNANI (?)

Fig. 128   15¾ x 11¼

IL CIGOLI

Fig. 129   15¼ x 19½

GIACINTO GIMIGNANI (?)

PIETRO DA CORTONA

Fig. 131   16 x 10¼

GIOVANNI DA SAN GIOVANNI

Fig. 132   5⁷⁄₁₆ x 6⅝

GIOVANNI DA SAN GIOVANNI

Fig. 133   11¼ x 16¼

GUERCINO

Fig. 134   9 x 8¼

GUERCINO

Fig. 135   9⅝ x 7⅜

GUERCINO

Fig. 136   11¼ x 8

GUERCINO

Fig. 137   14¼ x 9¼

NORTH ITALIAN, XVII CENTURY

Fig. 138   9½ x 7

PIER FRANCESCO MOLA

Fig. 139   11½ x

GUIDO RENI

Fig. 140

$50 \times 22\frac{3}{4}$

GUIDO RENI

Fig. 141   50 x 22½

GUIDO RENI

Fig. 142 $6\frac{3}{8}$ x $5\frac{1}{4}$

IL PASSIGNANO (?)

Fig. 143 $17\frac{7}{8}$ x $11\frac{1}{4}$

FRANCESCO VANNI

Fig. 144

$10\frac{3}{4} \times 7\frac{3}{4}$

VENETIAN, XVII CENTURY

ITALIAN, XVIII CENTURY

Fig. 145   9½ x 6¾

FERDINANDO BIBIENA

Fig. 146   7½ x 10¾

GIUSEPPE BIBIENA (?)

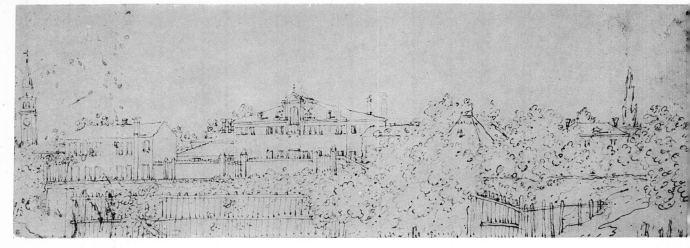

Fig. 147 $5\frac{3}{4} \times 15\frac{1}{2}$

CANALETTO

Fig. 148 $7\frac{3}{4} \times 8\frac{3}{4}$

CANALETTO

Fig. 149 $7\frac{7}{8} \times 11\frac{1}{2}$

CANALETTO

Fig. 150 $8\frac{11}{16} \times 11\frac{1}{2}$

CANALETTO

Fig. 151 $7\frac{3}{4}$ × 13

CANALETTO

Fig. 152   7⅞ x 11¼

CANALETTO

ig. 153   12¼ x 18¾

CANALETTO

Fig. 154   4½ x 6

DONATO CRETI

Fig. 155   12½ x 8⅜

GAETANO GANDOLFI

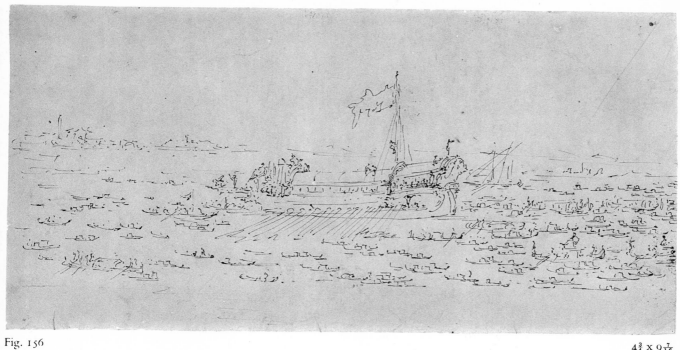

Fig. 156   4¾ x 9 7⁄16

FRANCESCO GUARDI

Fig. 157   5 5⁄8 x 12¼

FRANCESCO GUARDI

Fig. 158   8 x 3⅞

FRANCESCO GUARDI

Fig. 159   10¼ x 7¼

FRANCESCO GUARDI

g. 160 $3\frac{3}{4} \times 12\frac{1}{4}$

FRANCESCO GUARDI

ig. 161 $2\frac{15}{16} \times 7\frac{5}{8}$

FRANCESCO GUARDI

Fig. 162

ALESSANDRO LONGHI

Fig. 163 $9\frac{5}{8}$ X $12\frac{5}{16}$

PIETRO GIACOMO PALMIERI

Fig. 164   Actual size

GIOVANNI PAOLO PANNINI

Fig. 165

14$\frac{5}{16}$ x 10$\frac{5}{8}$

GIOVANNI BATTISTA PIAZZETTA

Fig. 166 $15\frac{3}{8} \times 12$

GIOVANNI BATTISTA PIAZZETTA

Fig. 167 $15\frac{5}{8} \times 11\frac{7}{8}$

COPY AFTER PIAZZETTA

Fig. 168   10½ x 14

GIOVANNI BATTISTA PIRANESI

Fig. 169   8⅝ x 6¾

GIOVANNI BATTISTA PIRANESI

Fig. 170   16 x 13⅜

MARCO RICCI

Fig. 171

GIOVANNI BATTISTA TIEPOLO

Fig. 172

$16\frac{7}{8} \times 11\frac{3}{8}$

GIOVANNI BATTISTA TIEPOLO

Fig. 173 $7\frac{3}{4}$ x $7\frac{1}{4}$

GIOVANNI BATTISTA TIEPOLO

Fig. 174 $8\frac{3}{4}$ x $5\frac{3}{4}$

GIOVANNI BATTISTA TIEPOLO

Fig. 175 $6\frac{3}{8} \times 10\frac{1}{4}$

GIOVANNI BATTISTA TIEPOLO

Fig. 176 $9\frac{5}{8} \times 7\frac{3}{4}$

GIOVANNI BATTISTA TIEPOLO

Fig. 177 $9\frac{7}{8} \times 7\frac{11}{16}$

GIOVANNI BATTISTA TIEPOLO

Fig. 178   13⅜ x 6½

GIOVANNI DOMENICO TIEPOLO

Fig. 179   11 x 7⅝

GIOVANNI DOMENICO TIEPOLO

Fig. 180   14 × 18½

GIOVANNI DOMENICO TIEPOLO

Fig. 181   14 × 18⅝

GIOVANNI DOMENICO TIEPOLO

ITALIAN, XX CENTURY

Fig. 182 $11\frac{1}{8}$ x $7\frac{3}{8}$

AMADEO MODIGLIANI

Fig. 183 $36\frac{3}{8}$ x $23\frac{5}{8}$

GINO SEVERINI

GERMAN AND SWISS, XIV, XV, AND XVI CENTURIES

Fig. 184   Actual size   Fig. 185   Actual size

ANONYMOUS GERMAN (?) ABOUT 1300–1350

Fig. 186   Diam. 9

COPY AFTER HANS SEBALD BEHAM

Fig. 187   Diam. 9

COPY AFTER HANS SEBALD BEHAM

Fig. 188

7½ x 12

JÖRG BREU, THE ELDER

Fig. 189

9¾ x 14⅝

ADAM ELSHEIMER

Fig. 190

Actual Size

HANS   BURGKMAIR, THE ELDER

Fig. 191 $7\frac{7}{16} \times 7\frac{1}{2}$

LUCAS CRANACH

Fig. 192

$11\frac{3}{8} \times 8\frac{1}{4}$

ALBRECHT DÜRER

Fig. 193   15⅜ × 11 9/16

ALBRECHT DÜRER

Fig. 194   17⅛ × 4⅜   Fig. 195

GERMAN, ABOUT 1480–1490   DETAIL OF FIG. 194

Fig. 196   Actual size

HANS HOLBEIN, THE YOUNGER

Fig. 197 $11\frac{13}{16} \times 8\frac{1}{2}$

HANS HOLBEIN, THE YOUNGER

Fig. 198   13¾ x 6¾

HANS VON KULMBACH

Fig. 199   Actual size

MONOGRAMMIST CB

Fig. 200   13 x 8¾

HIERONYMUS LANG

Fig. 201

$10\frac{13}{16} \times 8\frac{1}{4}$

HANS LEU, THE YOUNGER

Fig. 202   Actual size

GEORG PENCZ

Actual size

COPY AFTER TOBIAS STIMMER

Fig. 204

$9\frac{3}{4} \times 8\frac{3}{4}$

HANS·LEONHARD SCHÄUFELEIN

Fig. 205   Actual size

BERNHARD STRIGEL

Fig. 206 $1\frac{1}{4}$ x 1

WENCESLAUS HOLLAR

Fig. 207 $6\frac{1}{4}$ x 1

FRIEDRICH SUSTRIS (?)

GERMAN AND SWISS, XVIII AND XIX CENTURIES

Fig. 208

JAKOB–PHILIPP HACKERT

from Prof Lindner Col Leipsic no 798   Ph. Hackert.

JAKOB–PHILIPP HACKERT

Fig. 210 $6\frac{3}{4} \times 11\frac{3}{4}$

FERDINAND KOBELL

Fig. 211 $14\frac{1}{8} \times 20\frac{3}{4}$

FRANZ KOBELL

Fig. 212

$9\frac{1}{2} \times 10\frac{5}{16}$

FRANZ THEOBALD HORNY

Fig. 213   18⅛ x 25

ADRIAN ZINGG

Fig. 214   Actual size

ADOLF MENZEL

Fig. 215   12¾ X

ADOLF MENZEL

Fig. 216 $10\frac{1}{2} \times 8\frac{3}{4}$

MORITZ RETZSCH

Fig. 217 $10 \times 7\frac{5}{16}$

WOLFGANG ADAM TÖPFFER

Fig. 218   13 × 18

ADRIAN LUDWIG RICHTER

Fig. 219

$7\frac{7}{16} \times 13\frac{5}{8}$

ADRIAN LUDWIG RICHTER

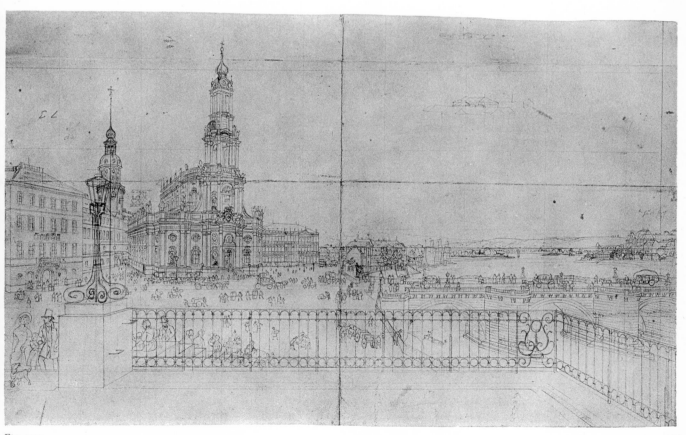

Fig. 220

$12 \times 19\frac{1}{4}$

ADRIAN LUDWIG RICHTER

Fig. 221 $11\frac{1}{8} \times 16\frac{5}{8}$

ADRIAN LUDWIG RICHTER

Fig. 222 $11\frac{1}{4} \times 19\frac{5}{16}$

ADRIAN LUDWIG RICHTER

Fig. 223   8 x 12⅞

ADRIAN LUDWIG RICHTER

Fig. 224   10⅛ x 16¼

ADRIAN LUDWIG RICHTER

Fig. 225 $12\frac{1}{4}$ x 18

ADRIAN LUDWIG RICHTER

Fig. 226 $9\frac{5}{8}$ x $15\frac{1}{8}$

ADRIAN LUDWIG RICHTER

Fig. 227 $8\frac{7}{8} \times 14\frac{1}{4}$

ADRIAN LUDWIG RICHTER

Fig. 228 $8\frac{5}{8} \times 12$

ADRIAN LUDWIG RICHTER

Fig. 229 $9\frac{1}{4}$ x $14\frac{7}{8}$

WOLFGANG ADAM TÖPFFER

Fig. 230   7½ x 9¾

WOLFGANG ADAM TÖPFFER

Fig. 231   9¾ x 5⅞

WOLFGANG ADAM TÖPFFER

FLEMISH, XV, XVI, AND XVII CENTURIES

Fig. 232   Actual size

FLEMISH (?), XV CENTURY

Fig. 233 $6\frac{5}{16}$ x 9

FOLLOWER OF BRUEGHEL (?)

Fig. 234

12 x 17⅜

PIETER BRUEGHEL, THE ELDER

Fig. 235

Actual size

PIETER COECKE VAN ALOST

Fig. 236   Actual size (recto)

Fig. 237   Actual size (verso)

CIRCLE OF THE MASTER OF THE HORTULUS ANIMAE (?)

Fig. 238

$9\frac{1}{2} \times 7\frac{5}{16}$

ANTHONY VAN DYCK

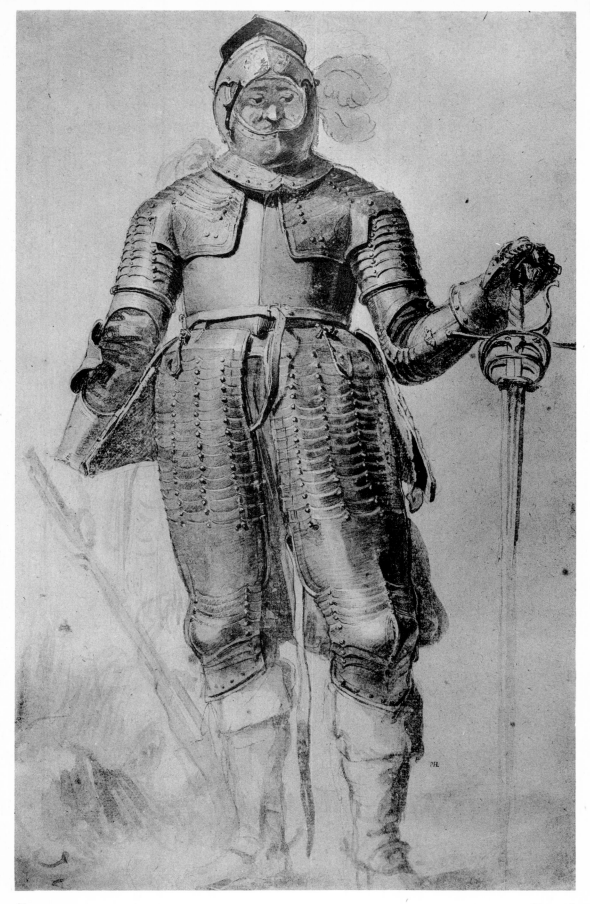

Fig. 239 $16\frac{3}{4} \times 10\frac{5}{16}$

ANTHONY VAN DYCK

Fig. 240

$14\frac{3}{4} \times 9\frac{7}{8}$

ANTHONY VAN DYCK

Fig. 241 $16\frac{3}{8} \times 8\frac{1}{4}$

ANTHONY VAN DYCK (?)

Fig. 242

$11\frac{5}{8} \times 7\frac{3}{4}$

ANTHONY VAN DYCK (?)

Fig. 243

$17\frac{7}{8} \times 25\frac{3}{16}$

GERARD EDELINCK

Fig. 244

$8\frac{1}{16} \times 9\frac{1}{4}$

FLEMISH, XVII CENTURY

Fig. 245

Actual size

FLEMISH, XVII CENTURY

Fig. 246 $12\frac{1}{2} \times 6\frac{1}{4}$

JAKOB JORDAENS

Fig. 247 $10\frac{3}{16} \times 8\frac{9}{16}$

JAKOB JORDAENS

13⅜ × 10

JAKOB JORDAENS (?)

Fig. 249 $15\frac{3}{4} \times 11\frac{3}{4}$

PETER PAUL RUBENS

$13\frac{7}{8} \times 10\frac{1}{4}$

PETER PAUL RUBENS

Fig. 251

10⅝ x 7

PETER PAUL RUBENS

$10\frac{1}{8} \times 7\frac{11}{16}$

PETER PAUL RUBENS (?)

Fig. 253

PETER PAUL RUBENS (?)

Fig. 254 $4\frac{1}{2} \times 9\frac{5}{16}$

LUCAS VAN UDEN (?)

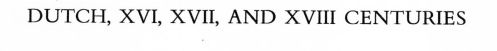

DUTCH, XVI, XVII, AND XVIII CENTURIES

Fig. 255 $10\frac{1}{2}$ x $7\frac{3}{4}$

CORNELIS CORT

Fig. 256 $13\frac{3}{4}$ x $16\frac{3}{8}$

ALLART VAN EVERDINGEN

Fig. 257   Diam. $9\frac{1}{16}$

LUCAS VAN LEYDEN (?)

Fig. 258   Actual size

ALLART VAN EVERDINGEN

Fig. 259   Actual size

NICOLAAS MAES

Fig. 260 $5\frac{5}{8} \times 8\frac{1}{2}$

JAN VAN GOYEN

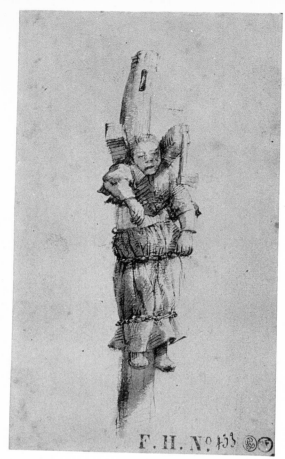

Fig. 261 $6\frac{1}{4} \times 3\frac{5}{8}$

NICOLAAS MAES (?)

Fig. 262   Actual size

NICOLAAS MAES

Fig. 263 $5\frac{3}{4} \times 7\frac{3}{4}$

PIETER MOLYN

Fig. 264 $7\frac{3}{4} \times 6\frac{1}{4}$

FREDERIK DE MOUCHERON (?)

Fig. 265

Actual size

ADRIAEN VAN OSTADE

Fig. 266

$7\frac{1}{8} \times 8\frac{9}{16}$

ISAAK VAN OSTADE

Fig. 267   Actual size

REMBRANDT

Fig. 268

$7\frac{1}{4} \times 9\frac{1}{4}$

REMBRANDT

Fig. 269   Actual size

REMBRANDT

Fig. 270   7 x 4

REMBRANDT (?)

Fig. 271   Actual size

REMBRANDT

Fig. 272

Actual size

REMBRANDT

Fig. 273 $3\frac{7}{8} \times 7\frac{1}{2}$

JACOB VAN DER ULFT

Fig. 274 $7\frac{3}{4} \times 11\frac{1}{8}$

WILLEM VAN DE VELDE, THE ELDER

Fig. 275 5 x 8½

WILLEM VAN DE VELDE, THE ELDER

Fig. 276 5¼ x 9⅛

WILLEM VAN DE VELDE, THE YOUNGER

Fig. 277 $3\frac{15}{16} \times 8\frac{9}{16}$

WILLEM VAN DE VELDE, THE YOUNGER

Fig. 278 $3\frac{11}{16} \times 8\frac{1}{2}$

WILLEM VAN DE VELDE, THE YOUNGER

Fig. 279   Actual size

CORNELIS VISSCHER

Fig. 280 $11\frac{1}{4} \times 9$

ANTHONIE WATERLOO

Fig. 281 $11\frac{7}{8} \times 9\frac{3}{8}$

ANTHONIE WATERLOO

Fig. 282 $10\frac{1}{4}$ x 13

DANIEL DU PRÉ

Fig. 283 $10\frac{5}{8}$ x $16\frac{1}{2}$

GASPAR VAN WITEL

FRENCH, XVI CENTURY

N.º 5

deborie

Fig. 284   12⅝ x 9¹⁄₁₆

FRANÇOIS CLOUET

Fig. 285

$5\frac{3}{16} \times 8\frac{5}{8}$

FRANCESCO PRIMATICCIO

Fig. 286   10 x 14⅛

RENÉ BOYVIN

Fig. 287   8⅛ x 7⅝

SCHOOL OF FONTAINEBLEAU

Fig. 288 $11\frac{1}{16}$ x $8\frac{1}{4}$ (recto)

Fig. 289 $11\frac{1}{16}$ x $8\frac{1}{4}$ (verso)

SCHOOL OF FONTAINEBLEAU

FRENCH, XVII CENTURY

Fig. 290

$7\frac{3}{8} \times 8\frac{3}{8}$

JACQUES BLANCHARD

Fig. 291   Actual size

CLAUDE LORRAIN

Fig. 292

$7\frac{1}{16} \times 10\frac{1}{2}$

CLAUDE LORRAIN

Fig. 293   6 x 8⅛

CLAUDE LORRAIN (?)

Fig. 294   Actual size

CLAUDE LORRAIN (?)

Fig. 295

$4\frac{1}{4} \times 7\frac{3}{4}$ (verso)

GASPAR DUGHET

Fig. 296

$4\frac{1}{4} \times 7\frac{3}{4}$ (recto)

GASPAR DUGHET

Fig. 297 $11\frac{7}{16} \times 7\frac{?}{?}$

RAYMOND DE LA FAGE

Fig. 298 $7\frac{3}{4} \times 11$

RAYMOND DE LA FAGE

Fig. 299 $8\frac{1}{2}$ x $12\frac{1}{4}$

SÉBASTIEN LECLERC

Fig. 300 $5\frac{7}{8}$ x $8\frac{1}{2}$

CIRCLE OF SÉBASTIEN LECLERC

Fig. 301

$13\frac{1}{2} \times 9\frac{5}{16}$

EUSTACHE LESUEUR

Fig. 302   5⅛ x 6⅞

PIERRE ANTOINE PATEL (?)

Fig. 303   8 x 12⅜

ISRAËL SILVESTRE

FRENCH, XVIII CENTURY

Fig. 304

$10\frac{1}{4} \times 16\frac{1}{2}$

CLAUDE LOUIS CHÂTELET

Fig. 305 $12\frac{7}{16} \times 16\frac{3}{8}$

FRANÇOIS BOUCHER

Fig. 306 $7\frac{1}{4} \times 11\frac{1}{2}$

CLODION

Fig. 307   6½ x 6¼

COLSON (?)

Fig. 308   14½ x 9

FRENCH, XVIII CENTURY

Fig. 309

15¾ × 9¾

JEAN–HONORÉ FRAGONARD

Fig. 310   7⅝ x 10¾

JEAN–HONORÉ FRAGONARD

Fig. 311   8¼ x 12½

JEAN–HONORÉ FRAGONARD

Fig. 312

$17\frac{1}{2} \times 14\frac{1}{2}$

JEAN–BAPTISTE GREUZE

Fig. 313 $14\frac{1}{4} \times 11\frac{3}{4}$

JEAN–BAPTISTE GREUZE

Fig. 314 $6\frac{7}{8} \times 8\frac{5}{16}$

LOUIS–FÉLIX DE LARUE

Fig. 315

$8\frac{3}{4} \times 12\frac{1}{2}$

JEAN–ANTOINE HOUDON

Fig. 316   Actual Size

AUGUSTIN PAJOU

Fig. 317 $10\frac{3}{8} \times 9\frac{1}{8}$

MAURICE–QUENTIN DE LA TOUR (?)

Fig. 318   Diam. 6

HUBERT ROBERT

Fig. 319 $9\frac{1}{4}$ x 10

GABRIEL DE SAINT–AUBIN

Fig. 320

$21\frac{1}{16} \times 16\frac{3}{8}$

PIERRE PAUL PRUD'HON

Fig. 321 $6 \times 8\frac{7}{16}$

CLAUDE–JOSEPH VERNET (?)

Fig. 322 $6 \times 8\frac{5}{16}$

CLAUDE–JOSEPH VERNET (?)

Fig. 323 $9\frac{1}{16} \times 11\frac{1}{4}$

CLAUDE–HENRI WATELET (?)

Fig. 324 $8\frac{3}{16} \times 5\frac{7}{8}$

JEAN–BAPTISTE CARPEAUX

Fig. 325

$8\frac{3}{4} \times 8\frac{1}{2}$

ANTOINE WATTEAU

FRENCH, XIX CENTURY

Fig. 326

Actual size

NICOLAS CHAPUY

Fig. 327 $10\frac{5}{8} \times 8\frac{1}{2}$

THÉODORE CHASSÉRIAU

Fig. 328

11 × 16?

CAMILLE COROT

VENTE
COROT

Fig. 329   11¼ x 8¼

CAMILLE COROT

Fig. 330

CAMILLE COROT

Fig. 331

Actual size

GUSTAVE COURBET

Fig. 332

11 × 9¼

HONORÉ DAUMIER

Fig. 333 $10\frac{1}{16} \times 6\frac{1}{2}$

HONORÉ DAUMIER

Fig. 334 $13\frac{5}{8} \times 3\frac{1}{4}$

EDGAR DEGAS

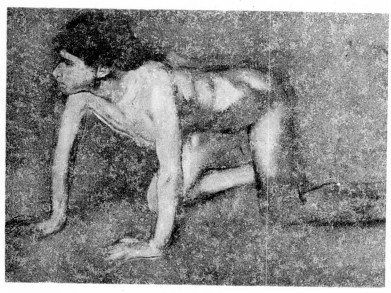

Fig. 335 $9\frac{1}{2} \times 12\frac{1}{2}$

EDGAR DEGAS

Fig. 336   16⅝ x 8

EDGAR DEGAS

Fig. 337   10 5/16 x 12

EDGAR DEGAS

Fig. 338

$9\frac{5}{16}$ x 16

EDGAR DEGAS

Fig. 339 $14\frac{1}{4} \times 10\frac{3}{4}$

EDGAR DEGAS

Fig. 340

$7\frac{7}{8} \times 9\frac{7}{8}$

EDGAR DEGAS

Fig. 341

$10\frac{1}{2} \times 5\frac{1}{8}$

EDGAR DEGAS

Fig. 342 $14\frac{1}{4} \times 9\frac{1}{16}$

EDGAR DEGAS

Fig. 343

14 X 9⅛

EDGAR DEGAS

Fig. 344 $12\frac{1}{4} \times 13\frac{3}{4}$

EDGAR DEGAS

Fig. 345

$12\frac{1}{4} \times 9\frac{5}{8}$

EDGAR DEGAS

Fig. 346   16¼ x 11¼

EDGAR DEGAS

Fig. 347 $22\frac{7}{8} \times 20\frac{1}{8}$

EDGAR DEGAS

Fig. 348

$17\frac{3}{4} \times 11\frac{3}{4}$

EDGAR DEGAS

Fig. 349

$17\frac{3}{4} \times 11\frac{1}{4}$

EDGAR DEGAS

Fig. 350

$17\frac{1}{8} \times 13\frac{1}{8}$

EDGAR DEGAS

Fig. 351 $28 \times 22\frac{5}{8}$

EDGAR DEGAS

Fig. 352

$19\frac{3}{4} \times 25\frac{5}{8}$

EDGAR DEGAS

Fig. 353 $31\frac{1}{2} \times 39\frac{1}{2}$

EDGAR DEGAS

Fig. 354

$25\frac{5}{8} \times 19\frac{3}{4}$

EDGAR DEGAS

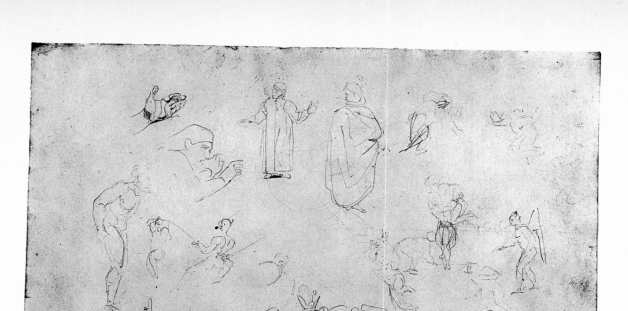

Fig. 355

$7\frac{11}{16} \times 12\frac{1}{2}$

EUGÈNE DELACROIX

Fig. 356

$9\frac{1}{2} \times 8$

EUGÈNE·DELACROIX

Fig. 357

13¼ x 9⅜

EUGÈNE DELACROIX

Fig. 358

$18\frac{1}{8} \times 12$

EUGÈNE DELACROIX.

Fig. 359   22⅞ x 15½

EUGÈNE DELACROIX

Fig. 360

$22\frac{1}{4} \times 15\frac{1}{8}$

EUGÈNE DELACROIX

Fig. 361 $11\frac{1}{4} \times 13\frac{3}{4}$

EUGÈNE DELACROIX

Fig. 362

$8\frac{3}{4} \times 7\frac{7}{8}$

PAUL GAUGUIN

Fig. 363 $9\frac{1}{8} \times 8\frac{1}{8}$

THÉODORE GÉRICAULT

Fig. 364

$11\frac{3}{4} \times 17\frac{1}{4}$

THÉODORE GÉRICAULT

Fig. 365

$13\frac{3}{16} \times 9\frac{13}{16}$

THÉODORE GÉRICAULT

Fig. 366 $18\frac{1}{8} \times 10\frac{7}{8}$

VINCENT VAN GOGH

Fig. 367 $14\frac{1}{4} \times 17\frac{1}{4}$

CONSTANTIN GUYS

Fig. 368 $7\frac{1}{2} \times 12\frac{1}{2}$

CONSTANTIN GUYS

Fig. 369 $7\frac{7}{8} \times 11\frac{1}{2}$

VICTOR HUGO

Fig. 370

$10\frac{1}{2} \times 7\frac{1}{16}$

INGRES

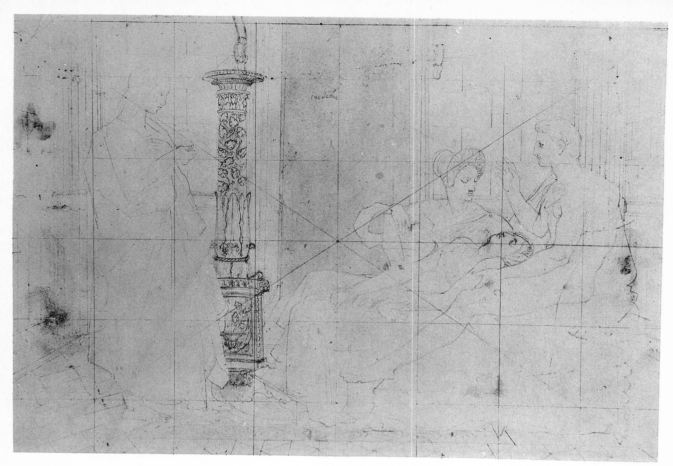

Fig. 371   11½ x 16¾

INGRES

Fig. 372   7¼ x 9¼

INGRES

Fig. 373 $15\frac{3}{8} \times 19\frac{1}{2}$

INGRES

Fig. 374 $15\frac{3}{4} \times 10\frac{7}{8}$

INGRES

Fig. 375

$9\frac{1}{4} \times 11\frac{5}{8}$

INGRES

Fig. 376   14 x 8

INGRES

Fig. 377 $8\frac{3}{8} \times 7\frac{1}{4}$

CHARLES-EMILE JACQUE

Fig. 378

$11\frac{5}{8} \times 15\frac{1}{2}$

EDOUARD MANET

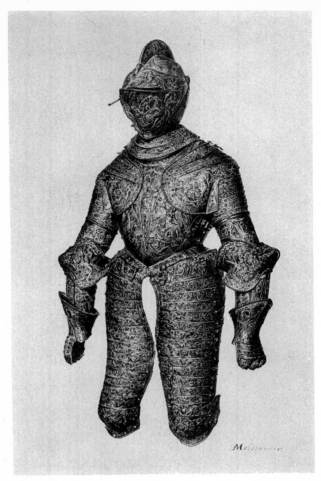

Fig. 379   14 x 8¾

ERNEST MEISSONIER'

Fig. 380   9½ x 6⅛

ERNEST MEISSONIER

Fig. 381

$12\frac{1}{4} \times 7\frac{5}{8}$

JEAN-FRANÇOIS MILLET

Fig. 382 $12\frac{3}{4}$ x 10

JEAN-FRANÇOIS MILLET

Fig. 383

15 x 17¾

JEAN-FRANÇOIS MILLET

Fig. 384 $8\frac{3}{8} \times 14\frac{1}{2}$

DENIS–AUGUSTE RAFFET

Fig. 385 $9\frac{3}{4} \times 11$

ODILON REDON

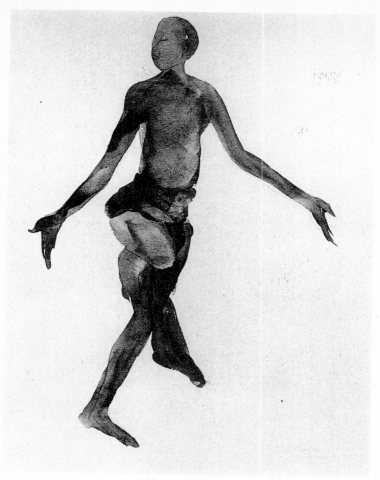

Fig. 386   13 x 9¾

AUGUSTE RODIN

Fig. 387   7⅝ x 8⅞

SUZANNE VALADON

Fig. 388   Actual size

FÉLICIEN ROPS

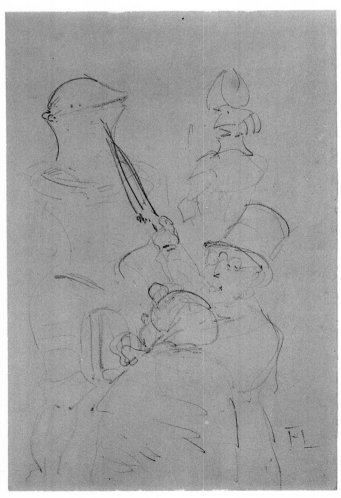

Fig. 389   10 x 6¼

HENRI DE TOULOUSE–LAUTREC

Fig. 390 $13\frac{7}{8} \times 9\frac{3}{4}$

JAMES TISSOT

Fig. 391 $6\frac{11}{16} \times 9\frac{13}{16}$

THÉODORE ROUSSEAU

FRENCH, XX CENTURY

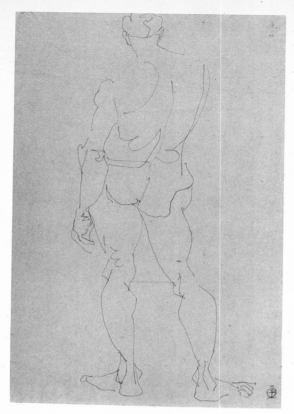

Fig. 392   14⅞ X 9⅛

HENRI GAUDIER–BRZESKA

Fig. 393   14¾ X 9⅝

HENRI MATISSE

Fig. 394 $21\frac{1}{4} \times 17\frac{3}{4}$

HENRI MATISSE

SPANISH

EPILOGUE

Fig. 395

Actual size

FRANCISCO GOYA

Fig. 396   12 × 15¾

MARIANO ANDREU

Fig. 397   19 X 13   Fig. 398   20½ X 12⅞

PABLO PICASSO

Fig. 399 $13\frac{1}{2} \times 10\frac{1}{2}$

PABLO PICASSO

Fig. 400

$9\frac{1}{8} \times 12\frac{1}{4}$

PABLO PICASSO

Fig. 401

$13\frac{5}{8} \times 10\frac{7}{16}$

PABLO PICASSO

Fig. 402

$13\frac{3}{8} \times 9\frac{3}{4}$

PABLO PICASSO

Fig. 403

$10\frac{1}{4} \times 13\frac{3}{4}$

PABLO PICASSO

MISCELLANEOUS

Fig. 404

$12\frac{1}{16} \times 10\frac{3}{16}$

EUGÈNE ZAK

Date Due